SOLO TRUMPET
and other B♭ Instruments

STARDUST
STANDARDS FOR TRUMPET
VOLUME FOUR

Music Minus One

6844

SUGGESTIONS FOR USING THIS MMO EDITION

WE HAVE TRIED to create a product that will provide you an easy way to learn and perform these compositions with a full ensemble in the comfort of your own home. The following MMO features and techniques will help you maximize the effectiveness of the MMO practice and performance system:

Because it involves a fixed accompaniment performance, there is an inherent lack of flexibility in tempo. We have observed generally accepted tempi, and always in the originally intended key, but some may wish to perform at a different tempo, or to slow down or speed up the accompaniment for practice purposes; or to alter the piece to a more comfortable key. You can purchase from MMO specialized CD players & recorders which allow variable speed while maintaining proper pitch, and vice versa. This is an indispensable tool for the serious musician and you may wish to look into purchasing this useful piece of equipment for full enjoyment of all your MMO editions.

We want to provide you with the most useful practice and performance accompaniments possible. If you have any suggestions for improving the MMO system, please feel free to contact us. You can reach us by e-mail at *info@musicminusone.com*.

MMO 6844

Music Minus One

6844

CONTENTS

ISBN 978-1-59615-833-7

FOREWORD

WELCOME TO STARDUST, Volume 4 of *Standards For Trumpet* and all other B♭ instruments which I'd like to sub-title:

A Seven Step Program To Increase Your Jazz-Playing Skills

In the previous three volumes, I touched upon these seven steps but now here they are prioritized:

- Sing and play the actual melody.
- Read and understand the lyrics and story.
- Play the actual melody, taking liberty with the rhythms and phrasing.
- Add ornaments and embellishments such as grace notes, slides, articulations and dynamics.
- Improvise connecting phrases but always try to return or echo the actual melody somewhat so as to stay "grounded."
- Create "new" melodies that have a similar character or flavor as the actual.
- Compose extemporaneously (improvise) anew!

* *You can certainly add an auxiliary exercise by writing down the fragments and ideas, and connect them methodically, or let's use the right word—compose—the material that you will later use on the fly!*

You must know that the great improvisors did some version of this, with some even following this method of writing licks down and "woodshedding" the many possibilities and permutations.

Basically stated, the goal is to install this information into our "hard drives" for instant access in a playing situation.

Okay, that's a brief explanation of my seven-step program. So now let's get down to applying them specifically.

The first song, **The Best Is Yet To Come,** perhaps should have been the last in this volume because it expresses a wonderful thing about music and being a musician, which is that it is a very fulfilling, life-long study.

In other words, you never arrive but are always learning!

This mind-set continues to serve me well and will do the same for you if you choose to adopt it!

You'll probably recognize this great Quincy Jones arrangement that Sinatra recorded in 1964 with the Basie band. I remember it well from my exciting days backing up The Chairman Of The Board in the 1980s!

With a complex melody like this that actually goes through several keys, it's **best** (no pun intended) to stay close to the actual melody and vary the rhythms only with an occasional ornament or embellishment.

Sound familiar? Sure, it's none other than steps 3 and 4.

Quincy's chart wasn't designed to be a vehicle for step 7 but rather a hard-swinging background for Frank to do his inimitable thing!

On to **I Had The Craziest Dream,** which is a very nostalgic song for me!

The most famous recording was by Harry James with the vocal by Helen Forrest. When I was a kid, I idolized Harry for two reasons: 1. He was, of course an incredible and versatile trumpet player and 2. He was married to the beautiful blonde movie star Betty Grable!

All I could think of was, I wanted to BE him, not only a master of the trumpet but in the movies and have Betty Grable in the bargain!

With this song, let's re-visit Exercise One, better known from previous volumes as the Opening Phrase Game and just for fun add an instructional twist to it in order to see how these phrases are actually chordal, scalar, intervallic and other dry music-theory terms like these.

Here goes with a quick look in this book at *I Had The Craziest Dream*'s opening phrase and what do we find but primarily a minor seventh chord. But what takes the exercise quality out of it is a lovely melodic fragment that provides contrast with a descending chromatic movement to the starting note. Yeah, I know I promised I wouldn't make this mini-course into the usual academic approach, but hear me out and I think you'll get something useful out of this. Just this portion of the OP (opening phrase) or with the lyrics, "I had the craziest dream," is a nice phrase/lick to imprint in your mind's ear-memory bank.

Milk this one by singing and playing it in all keys (you can randomly choose a starting note) and you will have a really nice phrase for your improvisational "tool-box." Remember to use the lyrics as a "GPS."

'Nuff said about that. Now it's time to bask in the moonlight of this dream-story with Nelson Riddle's lush arrangement. Enjoy the thrill of being able to solo with such a marvelous background, which here is actually Nelson's own hand-picked Hollywood all-star orchestra!

I do like diversity, and here's **Baubles, Bangles and Beads**, a great Rodgers and Hart song from the musical *Kismet*. However, instead of the original waltz format, this is a recreation of the legendary Sinatra/Jobim/Oggerman collaboration of 1967 where *Baubles* was cleverly transformed into a Bossa Nova!

I took the opportunity to sing Jobim's intro and overlay the trumpet to give it a more authentic Brazilian aura.

Just ride the gentle waves of this subtle rhythm, a sweet story that has a happy ending.

AND, don't be afraid to sing it first to "get inside the song," for, in my opinion, that's a secret weapon if there ever was one!

For a more classical entry into this volume, I chose the **Love Theme** from the movie *Cinema Paradiso.*

There are so many beautiful versions of this to listen and learn from on *YouTube*, including Josh Groban's and Itzhak Perlman's with John Williams.

I wanted to create a balance between them all using the flugelhorn to "sing" this with its warm, full, mellow voice. This is one of the loveliest movie themes ever written and when I play it on my live gigs, it invariably "strikes a chord" with the listeners.

The inclusion of **Can't Take My Eyes Off Of You** is a deliberate demonstration of how a simple pop tune of the 1960s can be rendered in a tasteful fashion. Though certainly not of the sophistication of a Gershwin or Porter song, it can still allow for a jazzy rendition.

My Funny Valentine is a favorite of mine as a straight-ahead slow jazz-ballad, and with this Riddle arrangement (circa 1953) that is at a considerably faster tempo, a different kind of flow is required. After the initial *rubato* section, it's almost a danceable fox-trot, to use an antiquated term, if it didn't go into 3/4 time at the return to the bridge. Again, keep those lyrics in mind as you play the melody and you really can't go wrong.

Before 1964, the music of Brazil was associated with this next song, simply entitled **Brazil,** usually performed as a samba. This version with a big band has little reference to its Latin-American roots!

In 1964 the Getz/Gilberto recording of the prolific Brazilian songwriter Antonio Carlos Jobim's **The Girl from Ipanema** arrived on the charts, edited to include only the singing of Astrud Gilberto. This became the first bossa nova single to achieve international popularity, perhaps the most successful of all time. The resulting fad was not unlike the disco craze of the 1970s.

A little more on "bossa nova" as a musical style: What is certain is that the term "bossa" was used to refer to any new "trend" or "fashionable wave" within the artistic beach-culture of late 1950s Rio de Janeiro. The term finally became known and widely used to refer to a new music style, a fusion of samba and jazz, when the now famous creators of "bossa nova" referred to their new style of work as "a bossa nova," as in "the new thing."

Back to Old Brazil and this swinging big band version which has little reference to its Latin-American roots! Watch out for the modulation into C concert after the marimba solo, the only suggestion of the original samba rhythm.

This next song is a unique and wonderful arrangement by Don Costa which was suggested by Frank Sinatra and is perhaps the only **Verse Only** recording in history. It underscores the wonderful legacy that Hoagy Carmichael has left us.

Here it's vital to really understand the story/lyrics while playing this melody instrumentally in order to get deeply into the beautiful verse of this classic song from the Great American Song Book, **Stardust**.

This classic truly stands totally on its own without the more well-known chorus, especially with Costa's symphonic treatment as a kind of tone poem!

Oh, Lady Be Good! is an example of the swing style sometimes referred to as the "dotted-eighth note feel." This great background track was recorded way back in 1953 with an all-star rhythm section as part of the first Music Minus One LPs (Long playing 33-1/3 rpm records for you young folks) that I owned in high school! They are now called Classic MMOs and are of course on CDs!

They are something of a hybrid of Swing and Be-Bop, but with a rock-steady pulse and easy to play along with. I used straight and cup mutes on this to fit into the time period.

Back to *Oh, Lady Be Good!* and the songwriter,

George Gershwin, who was a schooled composer. He was at home with many genres, not unlike Leonard Bernstein. He produced complex orchestral and operatic works and then shifted to popular songs for Broadway musicals and Hollywood.

With this song, he demonstrates his amazing versatility by crafting a very simple song much like his *I Got Rhythm*, which I recorded in Volume 1 (MMO 6841).

This has not been recorded often as a vocal with the exception of Ella Fitzgerald's big hit. There's a reason for this and I'm going to go out on a limb and tell you why.

First of all, don't bother studying the lyrics of this one!

What? Yes, I know, up to now I've been beating the drum for this device being the secret to acquire your jazz skills. So, what's with this sudden contradiction?

In my opinion, either the amazing lyricist brother Ira Gershwin just wasn't inspired that day or he was told to keep it **real simple!**

But the good news is **Oh, Lady, Be Good** is a fine song to explore from a instrumental standpoint and just like **I Got Rhythm** has always provided a basic structure for jazz players to do their thing.

I like to include what I call a "transparent" track to contrast the Big Band and lush orchestral backgrounds of the others.

I recommend that you strive for simplicity and space to stay in character with this song. To quote Benny Goodman: "Less is more." (Well not always.)

Music Minus One's illustrious president Irv Kratka, the founder and inventor of the play and sing-along concept that morphed into Karaoke, suggested I include a Christmas Song in this volume as I did with Volume 3, *Gold Standards* (MMO 6843). This song by Mel Torme had to be an easy choice, for it has literally become a standard! Its lilting melody and poignant lyrics are as expected and welcomed every Christmas almost as much Santa Claus!

Because most of this background is rather loose or more properly *rubato*, as is the *Love Theme from Cinema Paradiso* and *Stardust*, I recommend you listen a few times without playing. Even better: Sing along with the lyrics or at least hum along prior to picking up the horn.

Since the orchestra is not following you with a conductor, it's better to **wait** rather than **anticipate** as I did on the entrance of this song. Look at the transcription to see what I mean. It's just a matter of starting in this instance on beat two.

By the way, I was curious about the origin of the Japanese word Karaoke, so here's some trivia for you, it translates loosely as "empty track." Well, besides the renditions by professionals to follow as an example, that's what you have with the "minus one a.k.a. you" tracks available in this volume and on all of the high-quality MMO and Pocket Songs available on their website.

I wish you success in all your endeavors and if have any questions or would like to share any of your experiences from exploring the ideas presented here, feel free to email me at: *BobZottola@NaplesJazzLovers.com*

SOLO B♭ TRUMPET
(FLUGELHORN)

The Best Is Yet To Come

Cy Coleman and Carolyn Leigh

The best is yet to come,___ come the day you're mine. Come the day you're

mine.___ I'm gon-na teach you to fly. We've on-ly tast-ed the

wine.___ We're gon-na drain the cup dry.___

Wait till your charms are ripe___ for these arms to sur-round.___

You think you've flown be-fore,___ but you ain't left the ground.___

SOLO B♭ TRUMPET
(FLUGELHORN)

I Had The Craziest Dream

Harry Warren and Mack Gordon

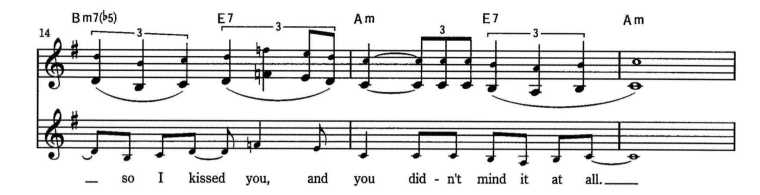

_ so I kissed you, and you did-n't mind it at all. _

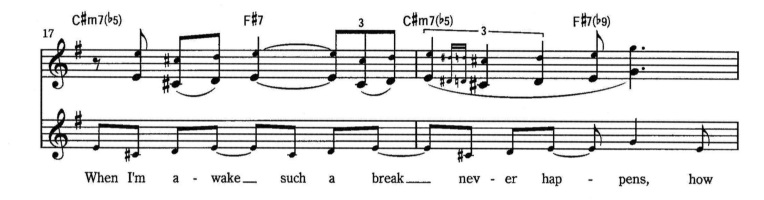

When I'm a-wake_ such a break_ nev-er hap-pens, how

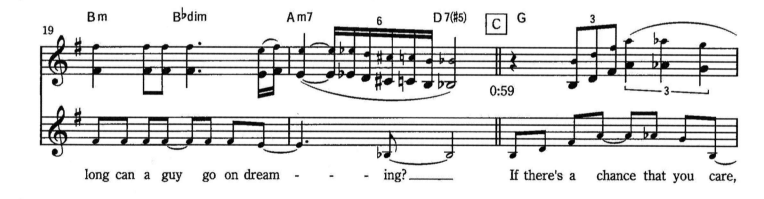

long can a guy go on dream - - -ing?_ If there's a chance that you care,

_ then please say you do,_ ba-by. Say it and make my craz-

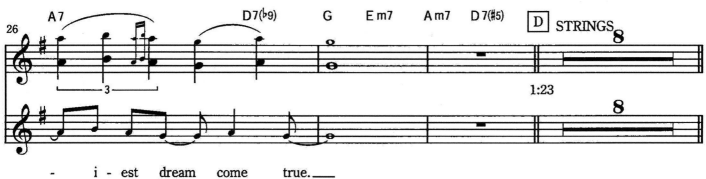

- i - est dream come true. ___

1:47

2:11

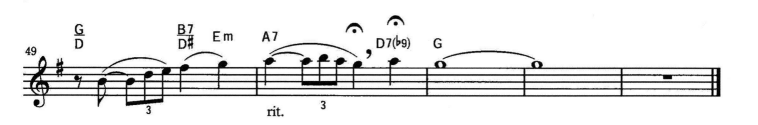

rit.

SOLO B♭ TRUMPET
(FLUGELHORN)

Baubles, Bangles and Beads

from *Kismet*

Robert Wright and George Forrest

MMO 6844

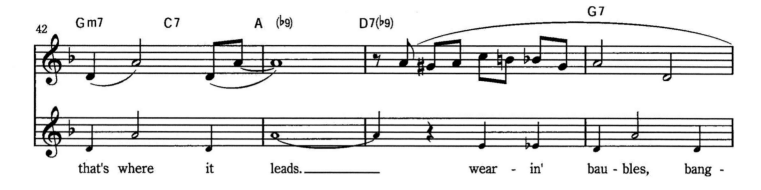

that's where it leads._____ wear - in' bau - bles, bang -

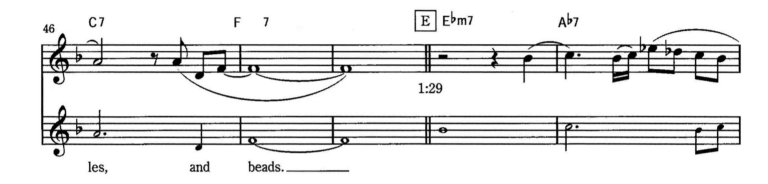

les, and beads._____

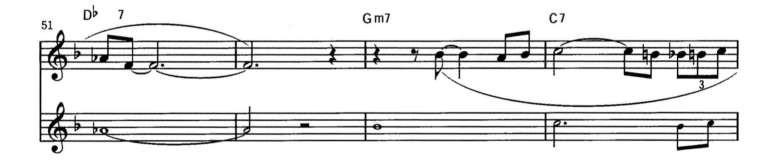

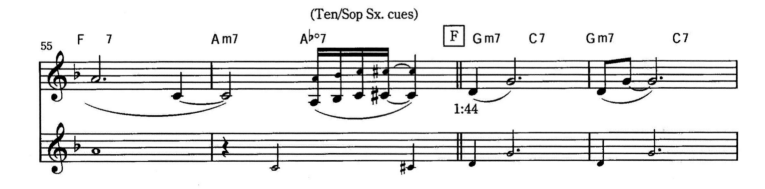

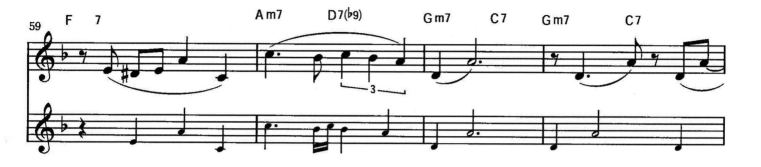

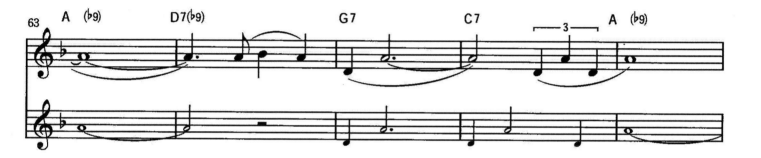

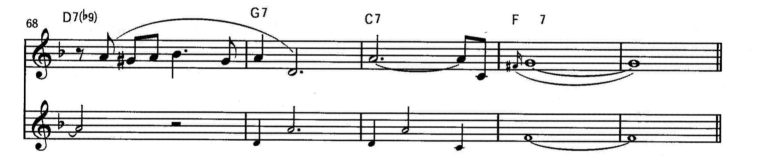

Cinema Paradiso

Ennio Morricone

Se tu fos-si nei miei oc-chi per un gior-no
ve-dre-sti la bel-lez-za che pie-na d'al-le-gria
io tro-vo den-tro glioc-chi tuoi i-gna-ro se'e ma-gi-a o real-ta.
Se tu fos-si nel mio cuo-re per un gior-no po-tre-stia

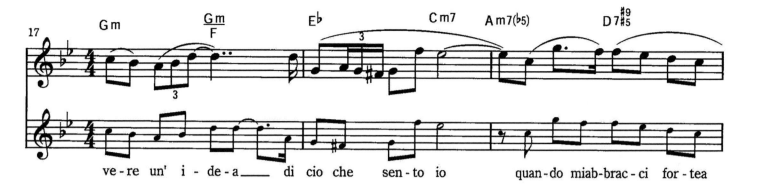

ve - re un' i - de - a_____ di cio che sen - to io   quan - do miab - brac - ci for - tea

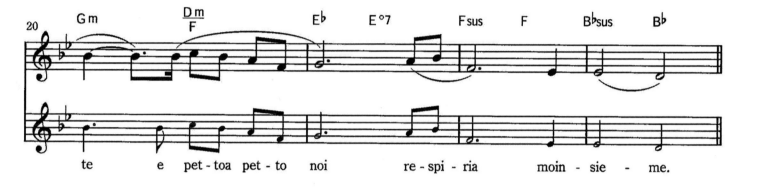

te   e pet - toa pet - to noi   re - spi - ria   moin - sie - me.

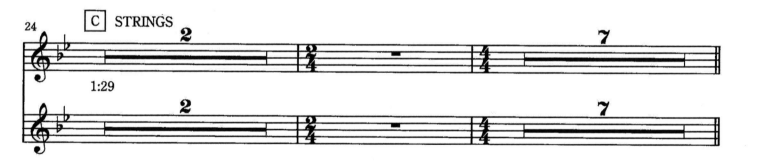

C STRINGS

1:29

SOLO

2:03

Se   tu fos - si nel - la mia a - ni - ma un gior - no   sa - pre - sti

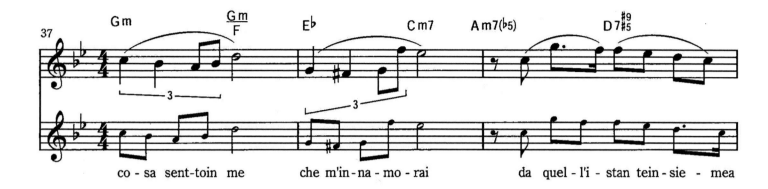

co - sa sent-toin me che m'in - na - mo - rai da quel - l'i - stan tein - sie - mea

te e cio che pro - vo - e so - la men - te a -

mo - re. Da quel - l'i - stan-tein-sie-mea te e cio che pro-vo

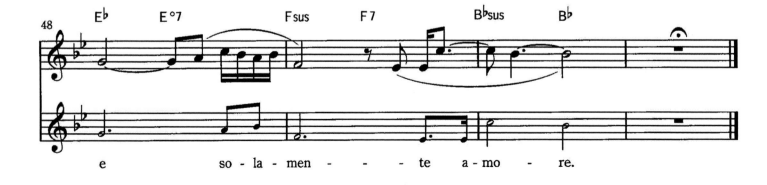

e so - la - men - te a - mo - re.

SOLO B♭ TRUMPET
(FLUGELHORN)

Can't Take My Eyes off of You

Bob Crewe and Bob Gaudio

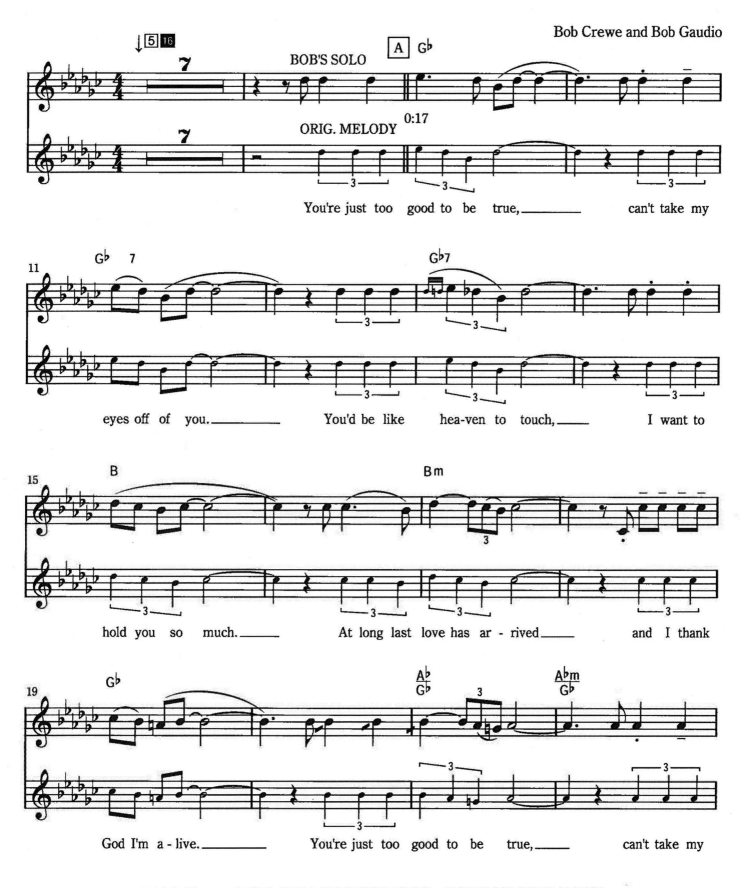

MMO 6844

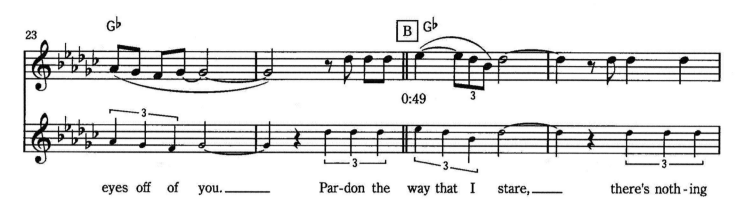

eyes off of you._____ Par-don the way that I stare,_____ there's noth-ing

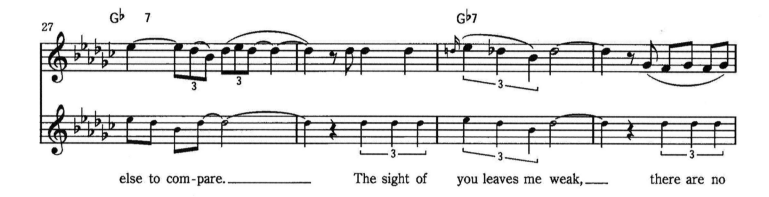

else to com-pare._____ The sight of you leaves me weak,_____ there are no

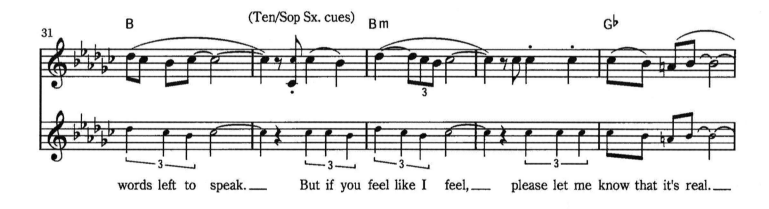

words left to speak._ But if you feel like I feel,_ please let me know that it's real._

You're just too good to be true,_____ can't take my eyes off of you._____

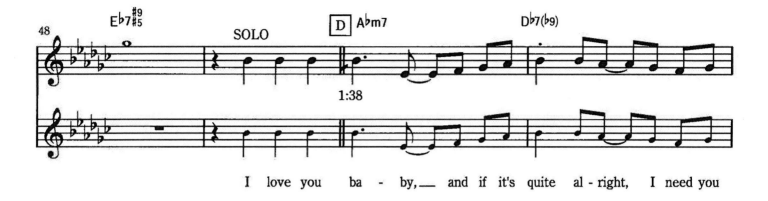

I love you ba - by,___ and if it's quite al - right, I need you

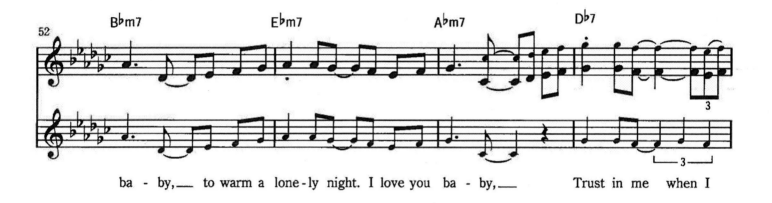

ba - by,___ to warm a lone-ly night. I love you ba - by,___ Trust in me when I

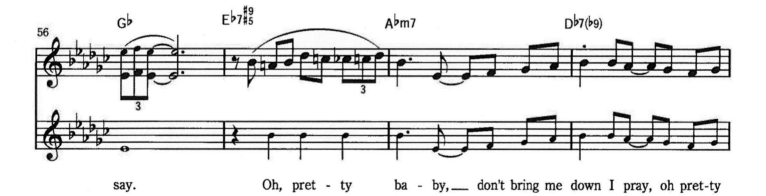

say. Oh, pret - ty ba - by,___ don't bring me down I pray, oh pret-ty

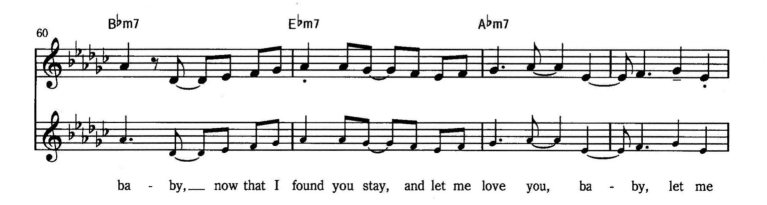

ba - by,___ now that I found you stay, and let me love you, ba - by, let me

MMO 6844

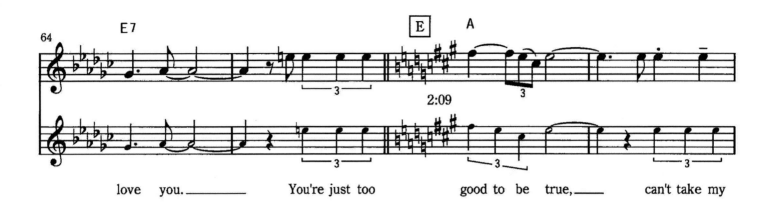

love you._____ You're just too good to be true,____ can't take my

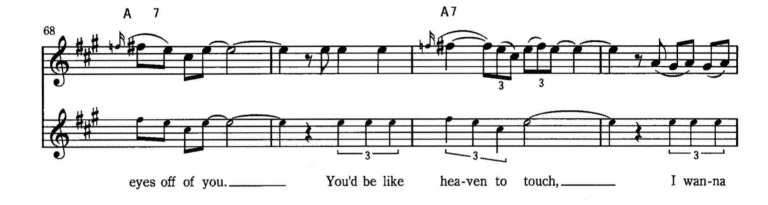

eyes off of you._____ You'd be like hea-ven to touch,_____ I wan-na

hold you so much.__ At long last love has ar - rived,__ and I thank God I'm a - live.__

_ You're just too good to be true,_ can't take my eyes off of you.__

2:40

I love you

2:51

ba - by, ___ and if it's quite al-right, I need you ba - by, ___ to warm a lone-ly night. I love you

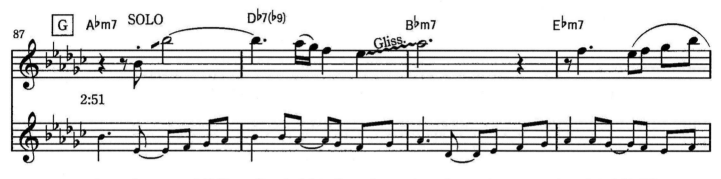

ba - by, ___ Trust in me when I say. I love you

ba - by, ___ and if it's quite al-right, I need you ba - by, ___ to warm a lone - ly night. I love you

ba - - - by, ___ Trust in me when I say. Oh, pret-ty

ba - by, ___ don't bring me down I pray, oh pret-ty ba - by, ___ now that I found you stay, and let me

love you, ba - by, let me love you. ___

SOLO B♭ TRUMPET
(FLUGELHORN)

My Funny Valentine

Richard Rogers and Lorenz Hart

MMO 6844

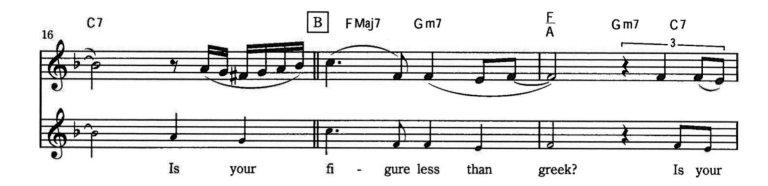

Is your fi - gure less than greek? Is your

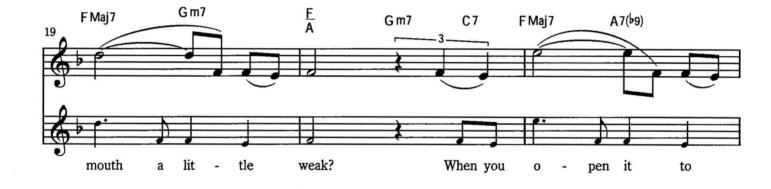

mouth a lit - tle weak? When you o - pen it to

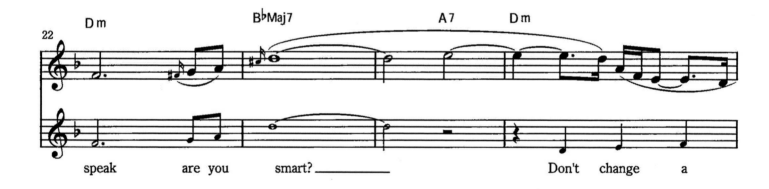

speak are you smart?_____ Don't change a

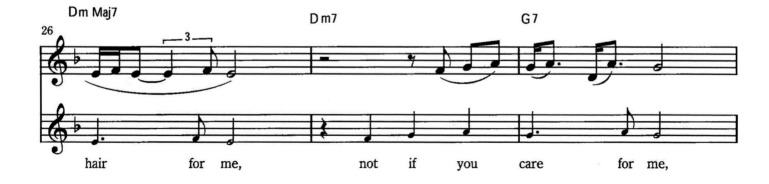

hair for me, not if you care for me,

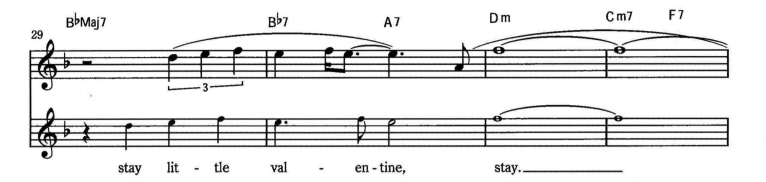

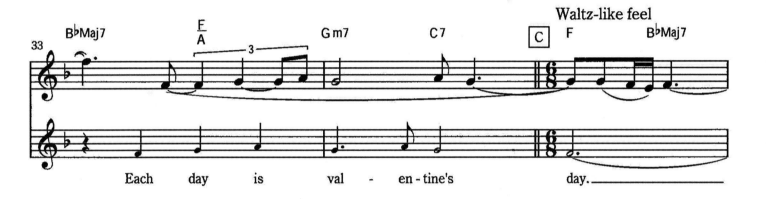

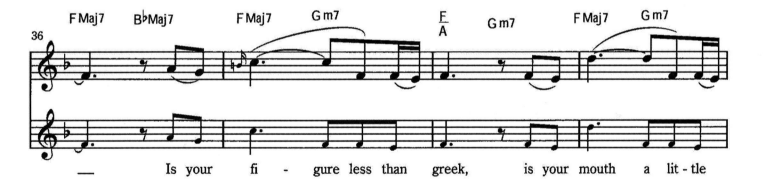

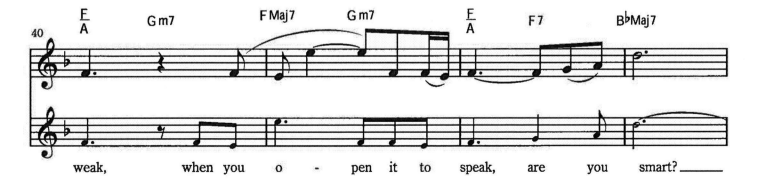

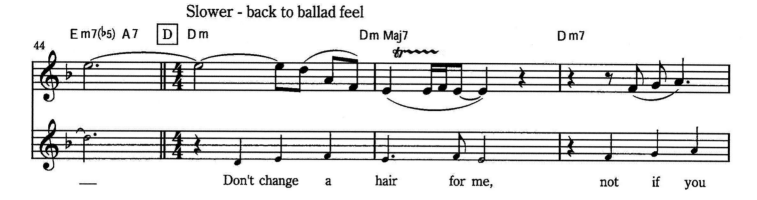

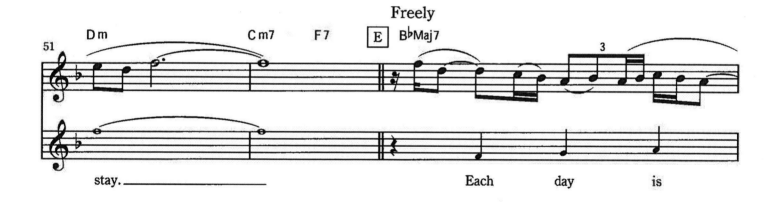

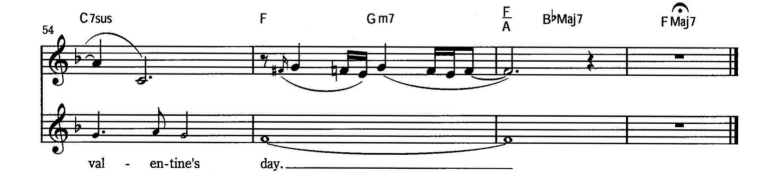

SOLO B♭ TRUMPET
(FLUGELHORN)

Brazil

Ary Barroso

BRASS

BOB'S SOLO

ORIG. MELODY   0:11

Bra - zil

where hearts were en - ter - tain - ing June. We stood be -

neath an am - ber moon and soft - ly mur - mured "Some-day soon"

we kissed and clung to - geth - er.

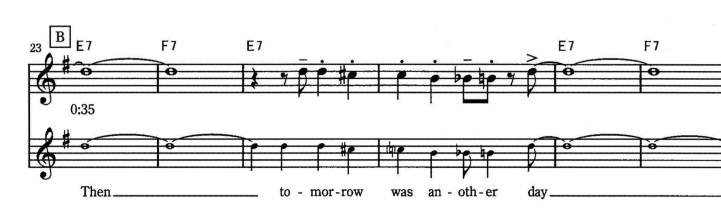

Then _____ to - mor - row was an - oth - er day _____

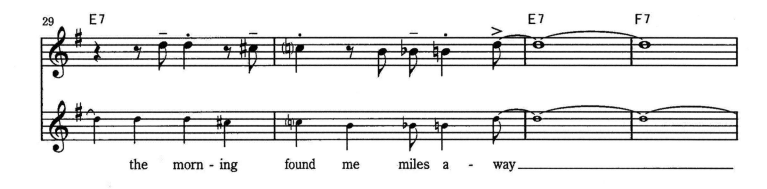

the morn - ing found me miles a - way _____

with still a mil - lion things to say. _____

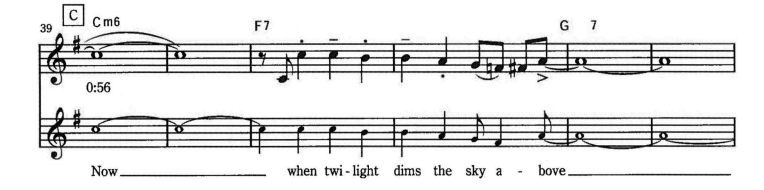

Now _____ when twi - light dims the sky a - bove _____

re - cal - ling thrills of our love.＿＿＿ There's one thing

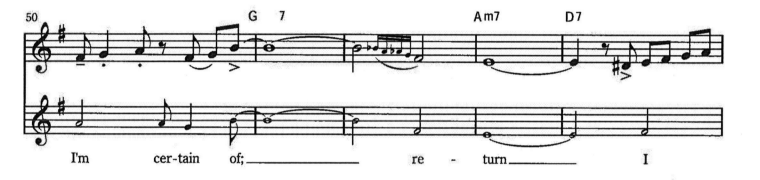

I'm cer-tain of;＿＿＿ re - turn＿＿＿ I

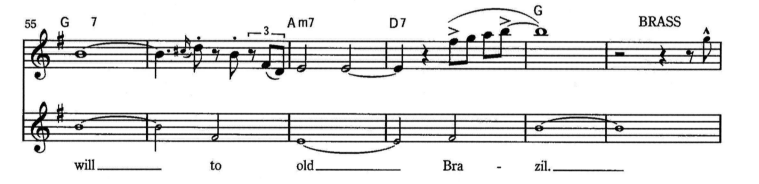

will＿＿＿ to old＿＿＿ Bra - zil.＿＿＿

1:32

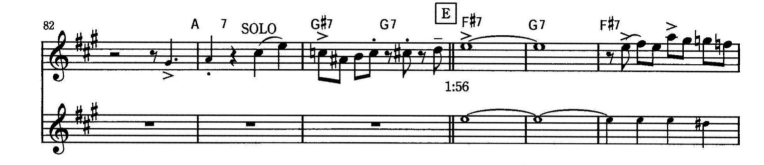

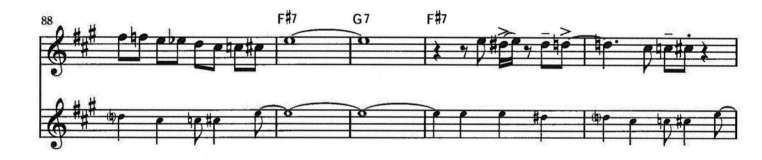

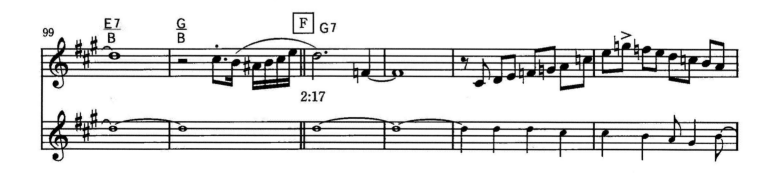

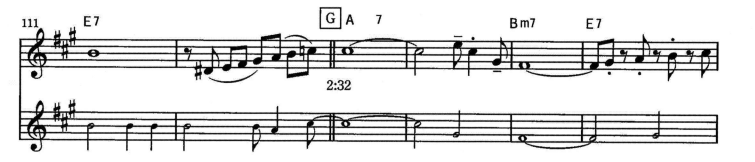

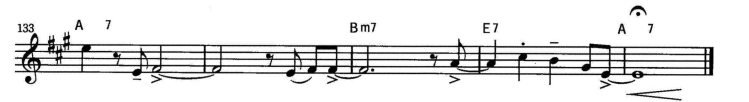

MMO 6844

Stardust

Hoagy Carmichael / Mitchell Parish

Lyrics under staff:

And now the pur-ple dusk of twi-light time steals a-cross the mead-ows of my

heart.   High up in the sky the lit-tle stars climb,   al-ways re-mind-ing me that

SOLO B♭ TRUMPET
(FLUGELHORN)

Oh, Lady Be Good!

George and Ira Gershwin

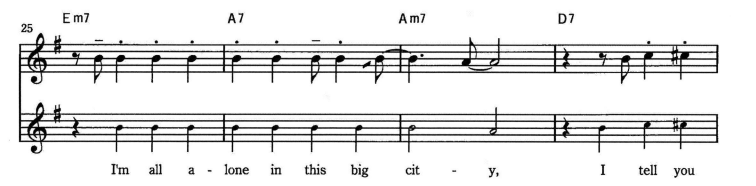

I'm all a - lone in this big cit - y, I tell you

I'm just a lone - some babe in the wood,_____ so la - dy be good_____

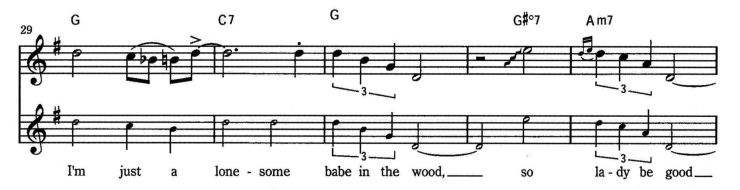

to me!_____

0:46

(Ten/Sop Sx. cues)

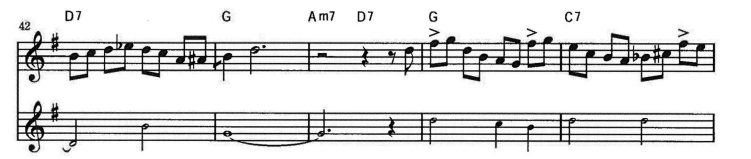

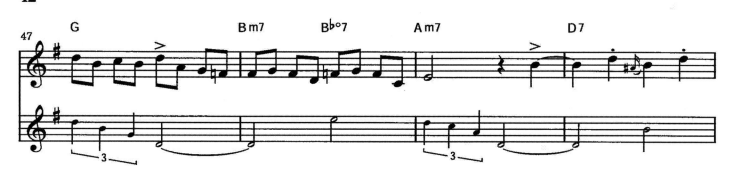

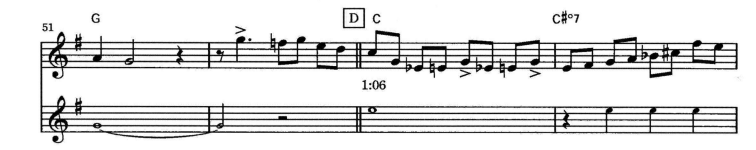

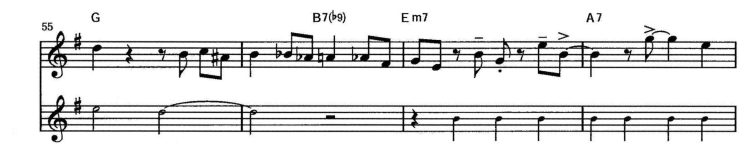

MMO 6844

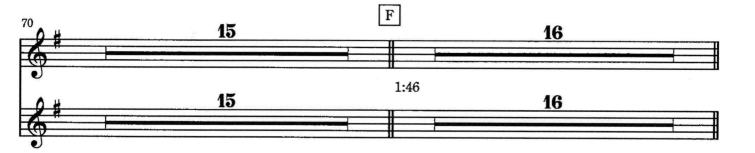

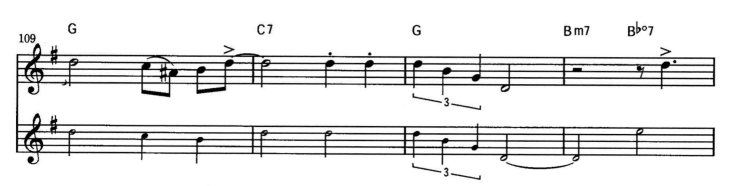

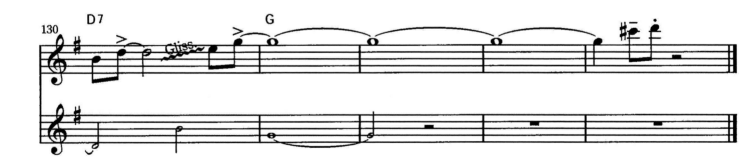

SOLO B♭ TRUMPET
(FLUGELHORN)

The Christmas Song

Mel Torme and Robert Wells

MMO 6844

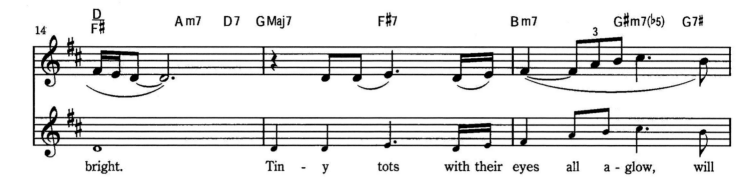

bright. Tin - y tots with their eyes all a - glow, will

find it hard to sleep to - night. They know that San - ta's on his

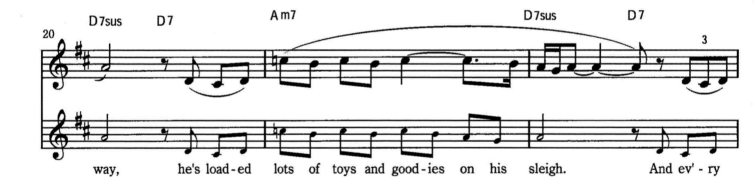

way, he's load - ed lots of toys and good - ies on his sleigh. And ev' - ry

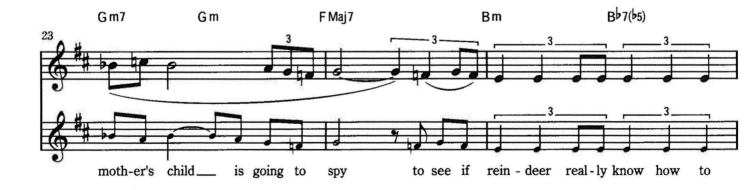

moth-er's child___ is going to spy to see if rein - deer real - ly know how to

Transcription and engraving by Joel Mott
jtldmott@comcast.net

MMO 6844

MUSIC MINUS ONE
50 Executive Boulevard
Elmsford, New York 10523-1325
800-669-7464 (U.S.)/914-592-1188 (International)

www.musicminusone.com
e-mail: info@musicminusone.com

MMO 6844   Pub. No. 0956   Printed in USA